California Beach
House Luxury

California Beach House Luxury

breeganjane

Written by Kristin Feaster and Terrence Dove

Editor Carisha Swanson

Principal photographer Ryan Garvin

Gibbs Smith

To Kingsley and Kensington

This book, this home, my entire life—they are all dedicated to you. I fought for years with all my heart to make this home a reality and a safe space for you. Go, be great, and create safe spaces of love, joy, and peace in the lives of others you meet along life's journey.

contents

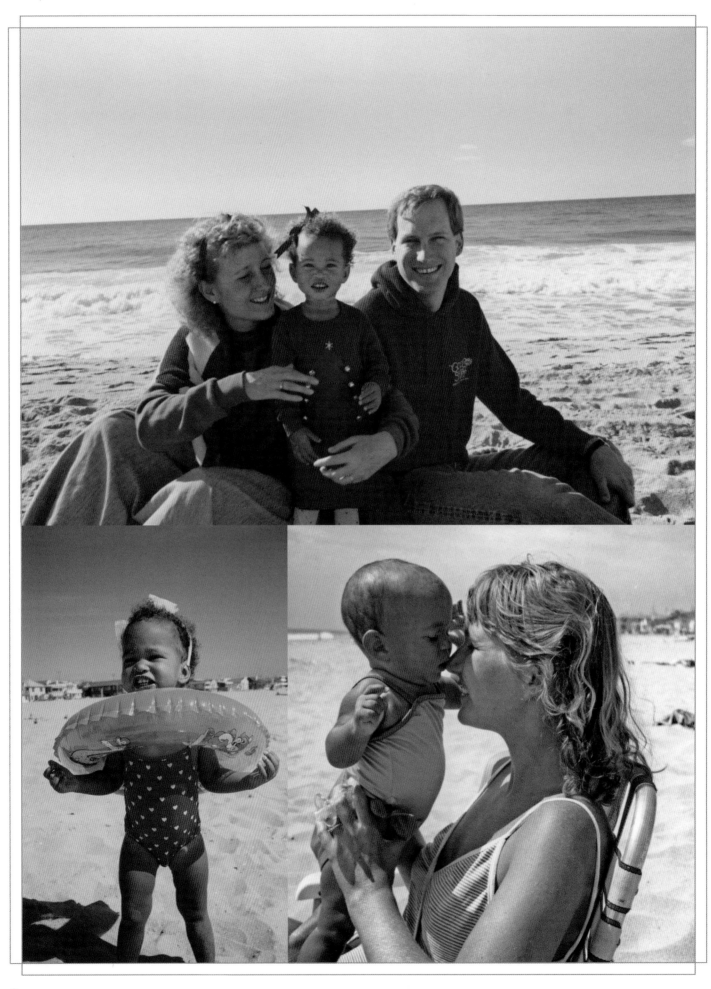

meet breegan

My childhood was spent with my toes in the sand.

As part of an almost daily ritual, my mom and I would head out the door to the beach, just across the street from our house, to enjoy the salty air and ocean breezes. The laid-back coastal neighborhood of my youth was two things at once—the perfect combination of unassuming and posh. Southern California isn't just where I'm from or where I reside; it's part of my soul and my design DNA and has been from the beginning.

I am the result of parents and grandparents who planted their seeds and grew roots in this region. The wafting of fragrant, ripened stone fruit growing in Grandma's Bakersfield backyard, and the sound of waves kissing the shore grace my earliest memories. How could I not embrace all that this quintessential California lifestyle offers?

My parents, both originally from Orange County, were in their twenties and living in the small beach town of Hermosa Beach when they adopted me, a biracial infant. Being transracially adopted certainly adds a layer of complexity to life, but my family handled the forecasted challenges extraordinarily well. There were never secrets around my "origin story." In fact, the undeniable differences in my appearance—my big curly hair and tawny skin—were celebrated. Being unique never felt odd among the members of my diverse community. It actually made me a prime candidate for child modeling, which I began at two years old. As a successful tot with a work permit, I booked major campaigns even as I got older, giving me the opportunity to meet and work with a host of characters in Los Angeles. My creativity blossomed, and soon I found more in common with the self-proclaimed "misfits" and eccentrics than with the suit-and-tie brigade. Venice Beach was brimming with quirky exceptions that dared to stand out. Tolerance and openness were built into the framework of my childhood.

The Golden State wasn't only home; it was my inheritance.

What is home to me? It's my sanctuary, my security, my serenity. It's a safe place where I can express who I am, what my heart seeks, and my individual style.

While my childhood dreams weren't necessarily full of decor delight, the artist in me refused to be tamed. Quite fitting when you consider my less-than-traditional *literal* beginning of life, the steps I took towards my career goals were anything but linear. When child modeling proved to be profitable, I eventually took the chance at entrepreneurship and opened my own retail store as a teenager. It didn't take long to discover I loved adorning the window displays and other areas of the store as much as, if not more than, I enjoyed creating designer clothing. That realization fueled my desire to further explore my passions. I felt drawn towards the channels that would help develop and hone my craft.

As life made space for my talent, opportunities to express the fullness of my creativity began to present themselves. One after another seemed to propel me closer towards interior design. I started styling interior spaces for an international luxury yacht brand. This unexpected but grandiose venture gave me the opportunity to meet a variety of people, and I soon began receiving offers to design for celebrity clients.

I knew this was the right fit for me when a movie producer, who was my boss at the time, challenged me to convert a steel, blank room into an office. With no further direction, I worked with audio-visual teams to make his vision a reality. Along with a team of forty men, I worked in an airplane hangar around the clock to achieve that goal. When all was complete and expectations were exceeded, I knew I was built for this. Soon after, my firm, Breegan Jane LLC, was born. For more than a decade, I have been creating "home" for families with the goal of encapsulating my personal lessons in legacy and love into places of refuge for others.

I've been blessed to call this my career for some time now. In fact, it was interior design that led me to another part of my career—television hosting. If my face looks familiar, it's because you may have seen me on Warner Bros. Discovery shows, Peacock, Food Network, or as the host of *HGTV Dream Home*.

A peek into a week of my life would likely convince the viewer that "busy" and "Breegan" are synonymous. However, nothing keeps me from my greatest priority: Kingsley and Kensington, my energetic and kindhearted boys. Of all the inspiration and revelation I find in my work, perhaps my two sons, with those big curious eyes, have become my greatest muse. As a single mom raising strong, inquisitive, creative young ones, I am inspired to pursue my passions—design, philanthropy, television, and more—for them and for me every day. I'm excited to introduce you to more of their effervescent personalities as we journey along in this book together.

My California has always been and is still a mix of surfing, peculiarity, and acceptance, with notes of glamour, elegance, and whimsy. Beach culture and all its unspoken rules permeate everything. With our proximity to the shore, we welcome wanderers coming in and out of our homes. Sand is always a main character, showing up everywhere. We hold a great respect for the ocean. We embrace that bit of rust and the welcomed patina that come with the salty air. These factors are simply part of our lives, part of living on the ocean. I intuitively translate these experiences into my personal design philosophy in both material and color choices. This is my "California luxe" life.

why california?

It's a legitimate question from anyone looking to build a forever home. But when you know California, there's no question.

In *No Country for Old Men*, Cormac McCarthy wrote, "Best way to live in California is to be from somewhere else." While I'm the exception as a born-and-raised Southern California girl, I get the sentiment. The Golden Coast, especially in the Los Angeles area, is an amalgam of global expressions that have meshed and matured into a culture all its own. My upbringing epitomizes a slice of the California way: a transracially adopted biracial child achieves her greatest dreams.

And I'm only one of nearly 10 million people in LA County.

If you dig into LA's history, specifically that of Santa Monica and Venice Beach, its foundations tell a similar story. The vibrancy of Venice's boardwalk and various amusements can be traced back to craftsman Arthur Reese, an African-American inventor from New Orleans. Charged by Abbott Kinney, the developer of the area known as "Venice of America," to bring diversity and inclusion to the city, Reese laced the city with creative artistry. Decorations included floats, gondolas for the canals and waterways, and a host of amusement park-like adornments. Though the city has burned down twice over the years, the artistry and wander-wonder of cultures flowing in and out of the region have remained, evolved, illuminated, and embellished its colloquial character.

That's why California.

Then there's the weather. I wouldn't be a proper Californian if I didn't mention how the Mediterranean-esque temperatures impacted my desire to build my ultimate home in California. It draws me back whenever I travel across the country. The grandeur of New York's cityscape always captivates me, but the winters never do. I tend to forget how much geography affects one's overall style and design aesthetic, but I am much more capable of handling salty air than frigid temperatures. While many dream of white Christmases, I can think of no better way to spend December 25th than with sand between my toes. One year-round season suits me well.

I can never forget the ocean: the infinite expanse that is my healing balm, with its rhythmic shoreline roar that lulls my soul into perfect peace and tranquility. I was born near it. I grew up with it and in it. I cherish it and find no better pleasure than waking up to view it every day. I am wholly connected to the ocean and vowed never to live anywhere it wasn't.

It is why California.

California personifies a love affair between the ordinary and the excessive. It is the beach and sun-drenched surfers, and simultaneously boutique stores and five-star dining. It's street vendors and electric bikes, skateboarders, and Muscle Beach. And it is Beverly Hills mansions and the bright lights of Hollywood. All of this is, and has been, my backyard. When combined, the aesthetic culminates into a style I call modern, approachable luxury. Think welcoming with a touch of whimsy, accessibility dotted with allure, on-the-ground practicality meshed with a bit of pie-in-the-sky.

The great thing is, while growing up and living in California birthed this in me, the vision and style it created are attainable anywhere. Achieving it is simply a matter of combining one's experience, essentials for living, and dashes of the exquisite. Whether you're designing a bungalow or a ski chalet, incorporating my modern, approachable luxury styling means creating an inspired, welcoming, true-to-you space that has touches of opulence throughout.

In my home, that is translated with a mix of materials, starting with both durable and manufactured stone. Upkeep is as important to me as beauty, so I alternate the stone I use based on the need. You'll also see hints of intentional imperfection in some aspects of the design. That's me, that's Cali, that's all of us—and that's okay! I think metallic touches visually elevate a space, so there are brass and other shiny selections throughout my home.

Cultural connection is a personal heartstring, so I've incorporated African and handcrafted artistry and influences within the scope of my design. They represent the people and land I frequent, love, and care for deeply. To further the spark of personal and purposeful design, I have employed custom furnishings where I could see opportunities. Since this is home for my sons and me, I want the pieces with which we interact to reflect our distinct preferences. Custom-made or not, intention is key. Everything is well-made, cleanly designed and calculated.

So, why California?

It just works for me. Venice Beach works for us. For all that it is and isn't, we can be our best selves here, and that's what anyone should be seeking when determining where to settle down and build a forever home. This area is walkable, which works perfectly for a family that loves biking or strolling to dinner, museums, and concert venues. We're near our family and extended village. From the amenities and location to the people and socio-cultural diversity, we are surrounded by who and what we love.

California is my north star. It is altogether my yin and yang. The cityscape invigorates me. The Pacific waters ground me. The culture inspires me. This has all collectively conceived who I am and continues to sculpt the masterpiece I will become. This home, the third house from the sand, will be the safe haven where it will all naturally manifest.

building the dream

first things first

We who grew up on Disney animations once believed that dreams would come true if we only wished upon a star.

Life is just that simple, huh, little cricket?

Don't listen to Jiminy. He's delusional and only exists in 2D animation. We live in the real world where any dream worth having, especially a home you want to live in, will require much more than a wish. One of the first steps is a solid plan. They say everything that exists was created twice, first in someone's mind and then with a blueprint. I considered several key logistics for this home to have before any contractor was called or nail hammered.

As you begin planning your home, think about this: if you're building a forever home, forever is a pretty long time to live in one place. Where will that be for you? You're most likely going to make a hefty financial investment in this venture, and chances are, you'll never be able to pick up the house and move it. It's an age-old adage in real estate that the most important factors in finding or building a home are still "location, location, location."

California provided me with an idyllic environment, one that I never see myself leaving. I knew I would always want to wake up to the ocean on the horizon. I will never not want that in my life. The location of this home is perfect for preserving this experience all my days.

The average homebuyer tends to think only about "now" when it comes to buying or designing a home. But what about when the kids go to college? Is the home you're looking to build going to feel the same as an empty nest? Will your home facilitate all you want in five, ten, or twenty years? Looking past immediate needs helped me inform several decisions about my home, namely an elevator and a ramp. They aren't necessarily mobile needs for me today, but what happens if mobility becomes a concern in my later years? I still need access to my entire home. Everyone should begin building any home with clear intentionality.

The last major consideration is to think of the things that unapologetically bring you joy. As a designer, I believe there is no way you can create a forever home without including things that will fill you with eternal happiness and inner peace. In my household, that's entertaining and being entertained. Dancing has always been a part of my life and always will be. I may have aged out of my club-hopping days, but my heart beats to any four-to-the-floor rhythm. I want the ability to start the party whenever I want, which is why I created my dancing bar in the kitchen. Fun is a requirement, never an option, in my home and heart. That had to be expressed in my dream dwelling.

I want to note that when it comes to your home providing you ultimate happiness: never settle for anything less than that. Fight for the things you want, even if they don't make sense to vendors or contractors. I encountered several who pushed to override my wants with their expertise. I knew what I wanted, I knew how I wanted it to look, and I knew the way I wanted things installed. Period. I could have given in a hundred times. When I look at my home and the particulars I pressed to keep, I'm so glad I didn't waver. Never give in on your non-negotiables.

picking perfection

Allow me to let you in on a little secret as you start your journey to find, build, or renovate the perfect home: it doesn't exist. What does exist is the home that is perfect for you. What is it going to take to discover that magical edifice? Patience and preparation will go a long way in helping you find the right home and avoid builder's remorse. Finding the best home is a marathon, not a sprint. The first house you check out most likely won't be the house you choose. Sure, it can be, but you should give yourself various elements and designs to look at for comparison.

Being prepared, especially with a professional real estate team, will provide support and accountability and will better guarantee you get the features you want. That's what happened to me. The origins of my owning this home came from the years-long relationship I have with my real estate agent. Knowing what I was seeking, he called me and said I should look at it. I wasn't looking for a home at that time; I was in escrow with another home in a different city. I ended up pivoting from that transaction into this home, and it all worked out because I was ready when the opportunity presented itself.

california construction

Take any Golden State anthem—from Katy Perry, the Beach Boys, Tupac, or any of the hundred others—and you will hear a beckoning, like a siren song, to make the West Coast your home. I would never disagree with that decision. The more, the merrier! However, there's a more realistic side to being a resident here, especially if you desire to be a homeowner: consider structures that already exist. Thank me later. You're welcome now.

In California, especially near the coast and in Los Angeles, it is very costly and time-consuming to build a new structure from the ground up. Our permitting and coastal commission laws can be challenging. My experience as a home designer has taught me that it is much easier to buy an existing structure here and take it down to the studs. I've trained myself to find property with great bones and excellent exteriors and work magic from within. That's what I did with this home.

The great thing about my home is that it was built by an architect who constructed the entire frame with steel. When redesigning a house from the foundation, it is important to be aware of the load-bearing beams

that may make it difficult to move walls in the space. I confirmed with two hired engineers that the frame as it was would allow me to build and arrange rooms the way I wanted. After their approval, I got moving, which brings me to my final consideration.

the dream team

In love and life, you have to be picky with your partners. Many of us learn the value of that lesson, for better or worse. If you're going to spend hours, days, weeks, months, and sometimes years with people entrusted to build the dwelling of your dreams, you'd better be picky! I won't let just any person into my home, and that includes my contractors and vendors. Neither should you!

For this project, I called in my five-star squad, my construction A-Team, to get the job done. I've spent years working with various home professionals and have curated the best of the best from those experiences. I continue partnering with them for my renovation projects. I know how they operate, and they know how off-the-wall (but calculated) I am. Now that we have developed trust with each other, those relationships just work.

Before I had this team, though, I made a point to get three quotes on every service needed. Why? Because whoever you decide to work with, especially when it comes to contracting, you're stuck with each other. Take your time and be slow to hire. Check out their work portfolios. Contact their references. Do all the professional background checks. Even if you fall in love with the work of the first person you talk to, get at least two more bids. You will want to get a good comparison of the work that will be done. After all, this will ultimately be your home, Goldilocks! It's up to you to make sure everything is *juuust right*!

And who should that team consist of? You'll definitely need an architect and a structural engineer. Your architect will help create your blueprint, and the engineer will sign off on the architect's work and make sure everything is mapped out correctly. Next, you'll need a contractor who will handle all building and framing. These people are your worker bees, so be sure to hire great ones! You'll also want to hire the professionals who will handle everything within your walls: the electrician, plumber, HVAC technician, and audio-visual technician. If you assemble the right professionals for this team, your home will be done in no time!

. . . well, maybe . . .

a note about deadlines

Remember the fable about the tortoise and the hare? You know, "slow and steady wins the race?" Tap into—and keep—that energy before you begin a project of this magnitude. It would be amazing if everything with a home build or renovation went exactly to plan and everything got done quickly and efficiently. The thing is, that rarely happens. Ever. When it comes to project deadlines for your home, settle in your mind to be like the tortoise. In home design, slow and steady will ultimately win the race and probably save you from getting frustrated.

There are so many things, big and small, that can cause missed deadlines or delays. Many of them will simply be out of your control. Those include city regulations, inspection issues, scheduling conflicts with contractors, and the list goes on. What can you do? Take your deadlines and throw them out the window.

Listen, there's just no science to deadlines. My rule of thumb is to take your realistic deadline and double it. Yes, double it! That's the advice I give all my clients, and it's the advice I gave myself. I planned six months over what I thought it would take to build this house. I took a year past that allowance. Focusing on the blame game will only produce more frustration. You'll spend more time on the past and not move forward. As hard as it might be, let it go. Move on. You will be that much closer to seeing your dream realized. That's the prize to keep your eyes on.

kitchen

These counters were made for dancing, and that's just what we'll do!

One person's culinary-creative camp is another's dynamic disco destination! If that sounds strange, it's because most kitchens are where the mouthwatering magic happens via someone in an apron with extensive knowledge of kitchen appliances. As a woman of many talents, of which cooking is not one, delicious dining might very well come in the form of takeout. But it will be consumed in the heart of the home, the nexus of social interaction. It will also be enjoyed in the sparkling ambiance of not one, but three rotating mirror balls. The experience is rated "extraordinary."

The kitchen, a space generally reserved for meal preparation and consumption, is redefined for me in ways as peculiar as they are magnificent. There is no feast without the fun, and my kitchen is the vehicle that gets us to the merriment, every single time.

double islands

While others spend delightful but reserved dinners around a dining room table, my family has always utilized the kitchen in more casual ways. The goal is always communal gathering and comfort, but at our most authentic, we stand at countertops conversing over occasional bites. Much like the cuisine consumed there, the space we refer to as the heart of the home is to be appreciated and reveled in. For us that meant incorporating double counters.

At one island, guests can use stools if they don't prefer to stand, while the secondary island has an eat-in layout and serves as a table. I'm an equal-opportunity, chore-giving mom, and trust me, nobody gets left out! That means making spaces accessible for my sons to help do daily tasks like setting the "table" for meals. Each bar sits at counter height—not only to allow social involvement among everyone, but so that no excuses can be made when it comes to sharing responsibilities. Pro mom tips and interior design, anyone?

mirror balls

You can't set the mood in any space without proper lighting, and the atmosphere in here is electric! Give me all the energy, excitement, and enthusiasm, and I'll show you a kitchen-turned-personal-galaxy, waiting to welcome guests with a shimmering light display that feels magical. The literal illuminating functionality of lighting just scratches the surface of this design choice. The trio of mirror balls, along with their scintillating reflections, is an homage to the floating paper Moroccan stars I hung over my four-post bed that was draped with curtains as a kid. The glow of the light would bounce all around me like a private Milky Way each night, evoking indescribable joy. I'm hoping to impart a bit of that same sensation in all who join my family in our countertop dance parties.

no upper cabinetry

Has there ever been as polarizing a topic in kitchen design as the "no uppers" discussion? While I wouldn't refer to myself as a minimalist, I do have a desire to have less clutter in my home and less space to store objects we don't need. Cabinets are utility-focused features, created to house and store. With my ever-growing aspiration to consume fewer and fewer shelf-stable foods and more fresh produce, upper cabinetry was rendered unnecessary. Design should tailor a space to the life we want to live as well as the life we live in the present.

The absence of cabinets in this space allowed for an even bolder design choice: antiqued mirrors. I was inspired by the classic French romance of the baroque design styling in the Palace of Versailles. The unapologetic gilded details and dramatic layers effortlessly usher in texture and grace. These diamond-cut antiqued mirrors offer a gentle reflection that perfectly complements the shimmer from the mirror ball lighting fixtures. With the front sliders of the house completely open and the beach and greenery on full display, the mirrors conveniently contribute to a serene and precious connection to nature.

brass sinks

Every parent of young kids knows the struggle of needing access to the sink, only to see it being occupied by children during the most inopportune moments. I sought to solve that conundrum and opted for multiple sinks with Kohler fixtures. With gained efficiency, my boys can have their own space when the other sink is in use. Double the sink meant double the requirement for style and refinement. There are two 33-inch sinks in the kitchen adorned with brass, my favorite metal. These beauties have a durable outer layer resistant to peeling, rusting or stains. The satin gold finish makes an ideal companion for the other golden-hued accents throughout the room.

countertop turned dance floor

"Dance like no one's watching." In Hollywood, everyone is always watching, but in our kitchen, it only matters that hips are wiggling and faces are smiling. Growing up in the city of bright lights, one could easily identify the star dancers in a production because they were often elevated, literally. That's exactly what I do with my VIP visitors: host them on one of the kitchen islands that doubles as a stage!

The island placement was a solution to a proximity challenge for the stairs. Realizing how close the staircase was to the kitchen, I decided to install two islands. The stair parallel to the island serves as the platform to get onto the stage when it's time to dance, a necessary aid as we all age and our "Hips Don't Lie" routines need a little boost when climbing onto tall surfaces.

Dancing isn't a special occasion in our household, it's just part of who we are. Moving the body offers a healing release, and our home becomes the entertainment headquarters guests never knew they needed. It takes socializing to another level.

music matters

Music is the great uniter, and I can't imagine my ultra-customized abode without a deliberate incorporation of one of my family's biggest passions: DJing. My sons take DJ and music production classes—and let's just say they might be rocking your next party sometime soon! We all believe the right flow of songs can bring positive energy to a group, so I didn't give a second thought to installing a DJ setup replete with the choicest enhancements.

No star DJ performs without stage illumination, so I designed the internal wiring for spotlights that would shine on the music selector. I also integrated a countertop bar with house speaker inputs to allow music to play throughout our home. The bar is aligned so the DJ faces the dance floor island, the kitchen audience, and the chef du jour. The space includes a booth speaker for monitoring while spinning music. When there's no DJ, the station will present as an extra stone counter in the kitchen because, after all, the layout will never sacrifice style or taste.

paneled refrigeration

"Cooking" and "Breegan Jane" are rarely mentioned in the same sentence; however, "innovative" and "designer" certainly are! I don't have to be a chef to understand the need for effective culinary tools that can create the delectable eats we enjoy. Nevertheless, I'm also of the opinion that refrigerators tend to be less than attractive pieces of decor in a kitchen. Though the typical inclination may be to shrink an unattractive piece down and make it disappear, I chose not to hide from it. Instead, I gave it prominence and weight, making it an intentional feature in the room, almost like one would design a fireplace.

I wanted the fridge to feel like a large, sleek vault, with amazing items inside it. I chose an elegant, manufactured stone facade that evokes a sort of magnetic quality, drawing visitors to it. The gray veining complementing a light-hued background over three 3-foot panels is, in a word, captivating.

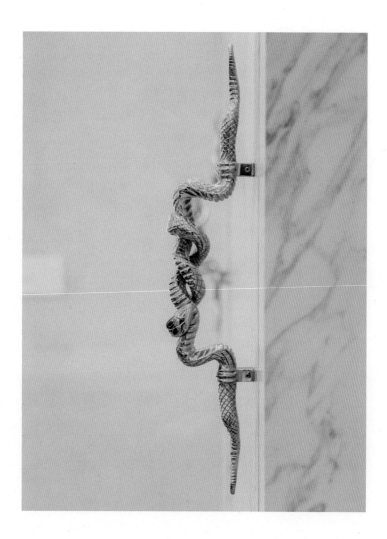

If I'm going to be opening my fridge to retrieve prepared foods for my family on a regular basis, I need a gorgeous view inside. This aesthetic demand, albeit lofty, was something I wasn't willing to negotiate. Enter a completely onyx-toned interior with LED lighting that showcases each individual shelf and compartment's framework, balancing the sable sophistication with luxurious illumination throughout. I'd say we surpassed the beauty standard.

Boasting nearly silent volumes, the refrigerator hails as one of the quietest luxury appliances out. It also supports sustainability efforts, as the columns have options to avoid sudden changes in temperature and humidity. There are options to adjust the power while you're on vacation. Tantalizing and energy-conserving, this appliance speaks to the needs of today and tomorrow, which I sincerely appreciate.

a range beyond

Traditional has never quite been my style, so why start now? The 48-inch dual-fuel range with a downdraft vent, chrome-infused griddle, and steam assist isn't just brimming with technological conveniences and superior engineering; it's also a showstopper, featuring my signature mixed metals. The range has brass knob collars and geometric grates. The knobs also feature a ring of LED lights that glow when the oven is on. More than an essential element of any kitchen, this range is appliance-turned-art. With all that visual charisma, I couldn't bear to give this beauty a conventional corner or wall placement. The kitchen was designed to be a cavernous and open space, so I stationed the range towards the center of the kitchen in one of the islands. This configuration allows the cook to face the entire room as well as this stunner of a device.

living
room

For me, the living room is a space of community and casual conversation for family, friends, and guests alike. I travel often for work and play, so those moments of connecting don't happen as often as I'd like. That's why seating was a primary focus as I began designing my living room. It needed to facilitate as much engagement as possible.

Because of my hectic travel schedule, I fashioned my living room design around one of the places I often frequent: airport lobbies. This may seem like an odd place to look for design inspiration, but the seating in lobbies strongly appeals to my sense of engagement with family and friends. Lounges primarily utilize individual seating to accommodate multiple people and travelers comfortably. In my home, I rearranged the seating to allow guests to face each other. If I'm privileged enough to get the juicy details of a friend's new beau, I want to lock in with eyes and ears, with nothing in the way of discovering everything!

I opted for four circular chairs because they're extremely comfortable, lightweight, and easy to reconfigure on a whim. Though you rarely see a couch in an airport, I wanted a place in our home where the boys and I could cuddle up and watch movies together. I commissioned a built-in couch that resembles more of an oversized daybed. There is ample space for all of us, and it adds to the relaxing aesthetic created by the rest of the room's design.

All in all, our living room is not traditional, but it creates the perfect environment that makes us feel right at home.

pedestal table

Our "drop zone" is the pedestal table I commissioned from Arts Out of Africa. I fell in love with this when I saw some other custom furniture they created and knew I needed a personalized item in this forever home. The hand has several symbolic meanings: I work primarily with my hands as a designer, and all I do holds up my family and my life goals. This table presents the perfect welcome to my family and guests as they enter the living room.

music corner

As a musical and artful family, we had to have additional elements that felt fully like us. The baby grand piano sits in a corner designed for it. This is where the boys tickle the ivories with a few rounds of "Chopsticks." Its creamy white enhances the neutral foundation and visuals throughout the home. Will my sons become master pianists? Only time will tell. But they'll always have their piano to practice on if they do.

fireplace and nook

Stone has the power to create an instant vision of elegance and luxury in a home. The fireplace is made of a marbled sintered stone that goes from the floor to the ceiling. The material mimics aspects of nature and is just as calming. I love ushering in that feeling in interior spaces. Keeping with the cozy motif, I decided to maintain the heated floors from the original plan; warm floors provide an unexpected sensation that cooler floors do not.

I always lean towards elements of surprise, and in this home it was a nook for meditation and reading. That particular space was originally slated to house Citrine, my sons' pet ball python (I know, I know, but this is the family pet!). A second thought led me to design the area with a more intimate, repose-focused ambiance.

The nook entrance is draped in beads that add a hint of seclusion and privacy. To keep it super cozy, I loaded it up with cushy pillows that provide extra comfort and relaxing vibes. Who wouldn't want to hide away here for a few hours? This is a great spot for my kids because I taught them to meditate when they need to calm down and center themselves—so I don't have to do it for them and then have to calm myself down! Win-win. Since I wanted the nook to be a floating space, I commissioned Phillips Collection to create stone "steps" to help everyone get into the meditation nook. I love the custom look because the steps, made from petrified wood, look like they were made for this exact purpose.

family patio

Living in sunny Los Angeles, our outdoor space is totally an extension of our indoor space, and in my neighborhood people's patios are the ultimate connection to community. Growing up, it was like that too. We would open our doors, and people we sometimes hadn't seen for years would yell up to say "hello" and stop by for a few moments on their way to the beach. In a tight-knit community like ours, sitting on your rooftop or patio is an inevitable invitation for neighborly greetings and company.

With the slider doors open and everything beyond them within earshot, the elevated patio is instantly connected to the lower level at the front of the house. The greenery outside and the salty air that wafts through both become as much a part of the home as the decor right inside those doors. Even from my kitchen, I can hear the kids playing outside, the local running club whizzing by, and the surfers sprinting out to the shore. The patio in some strangely beautiful way serves as a bond to the people around us who share our adjacent spaces and similar lifestyles. That link is a hallmark of this area, and the patio is what grants it to us.

citrine

My kids wanted a dog, so I bought them a snake.

Citrine, aptly named for the lemony quartz with which she shares her coloring, is our pet ball python. She is also the cause of many gasps and looks of shock when we introduce her to our friends. Why do we have a pet snake? Well, we are a family that values travel, and for several parts of the year we find ourselves away more than at home. I wanted to give my sons the experience of having a pet; however, low maintenance was a must.

I was a girly-girl, but I grew up with reptiles like lizards and snakes. I am repeating that with my own children. We have had Citrine for three years, and she practically watched the house being built right along with us. She's a surprise to most people who meet her, but our cuddle-bug movie-watcher (she really does!) of a snake is perfectly normal for us! Citrine is a part of our family, and where you find us, you'll likely see her.

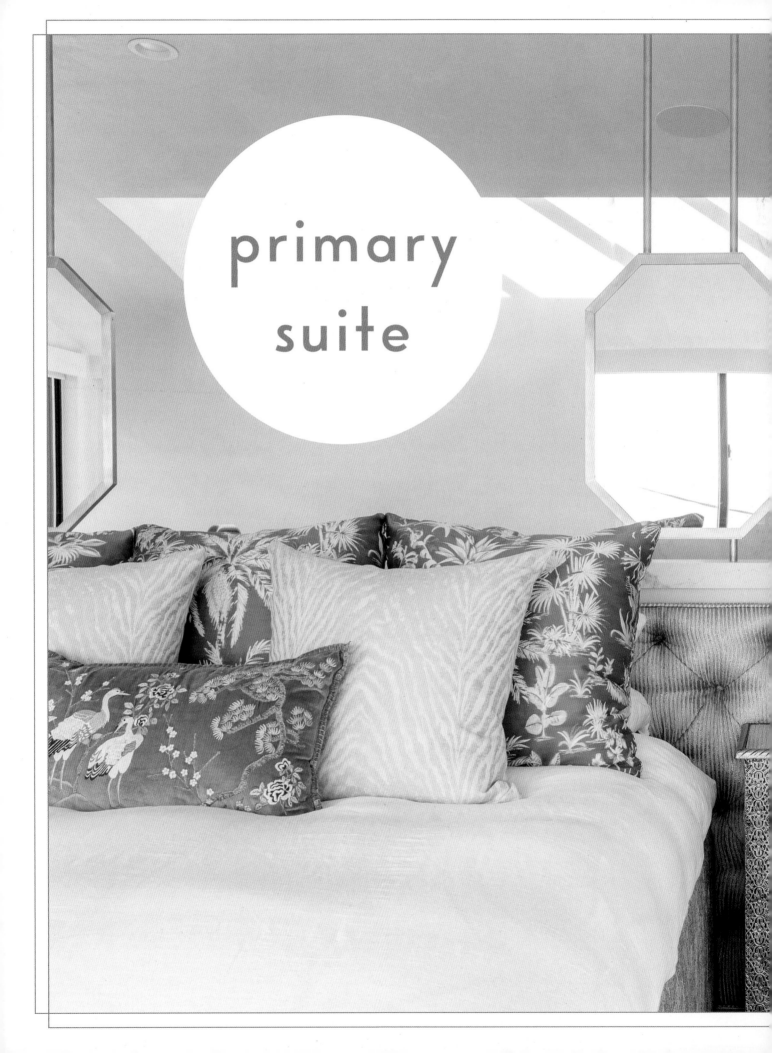

primary
suite

Have you ever heard Diana Ross's song "It's My House"? It's a great 1979 R&B track in which she details everything that makes her house a home. From the table to the ceiling to the shelves and stairs, Ms. Ross explains that every element in her home was built out of and for love. Let's pause right here and catch her vibe. Grab your mobile device, find your favorite music platform and give it a listen. I'm a DJ; I promise I won't steer you wrong.

Go, do it. *Right now*! I'll wait.

Awesome tune, right? I love how Ms. Ross made the home welcoming for others, but she lets you know in no uncertain terms that this is her space. I completely get that. My home was created to be a place for gathering. But everyone here needs a place of repose suited just for them. The private primary bedroom—my bedroom—is a quintessential Breegan space. The layout, design, and features unify to create my ultimate place of comfort, tranquility, and reprieve—bliss.

Aside from needing a private place of retreat, I wanted a space that would allow me to bask in the elements of nature with which I connect most: the sun and ocean. Since this is on the highest level in the home, it was a no-brainer to capitalize on the picturesque viewscape.

Both the bedroom and the adjacent bathroom intentionally face west, toward the Pacific Ocean. I count it a privilege and honor to wake up to the sea-foam and waves each morning and relish the ethereal sun as it sets each day. I'll never tire of that. It is the exact scene I enjoyed over and over as a young girl, then as a teenager, and now an adult. And it is still a marvel.

the entrance

I am mostly a social being. Ninety-five percent of my home is dedicated to having fun with my boys and guests. But that other five percent— my primary bedroom and bathroom—is reserved solely for me. Perhaps the best feature is its exclusivity. I incorporated a private internal staircase with an access point marked by a stately Moroccan door. I chose to have doors with brass overlay shipped from Morocco to pay homage to the richness of African culture I adore, as well as to preface the luxury that awaits up the stairs.

This stunning entryway also serves as my bedroom's personal VIP access. The door's lock mechanism engages automatically whenever it closes. Guests desiring access to the inner domain will need to be buzzed in by me. I had an entrance buzzer installed in the headboard of my custom bed that notifies me of anyone beckoning to enter. And only I get to make that decision. When it comes to my inner lair, I'm the beauty and the bouncer in one! It's my unique way of protecting my personal peace and my private "pretty."

custom headboard

Immediately after ascending the stairs, one encounters the crown jewel of the space—
my California King bed, centered in the room. Listen, it's a showstopper! The custom
headboard and sideboard coverings are from my fabric line with Clarke and Clarke
Interiors. The Kalya print, meshing hints of gold with luxe linen textures, adds tailor-
made singularity to the bed and overall presentation. What's more, the design artistically
reflects the horizon I wake up to and lie down to each night. I love that I get to wrap up in
it when I settle down. It's the epitome of luxury.

screen time

The irony of being a television personality is that my life doesn't allow many moments to veg on television shows for hours on end. But honestly, who am I kidding? I'd much rather be on the red carpet than watching it from the sidelines. Still, I'm a designer who believes no room should be without its digital entertainment luxuries. I wanted the option to have on-demand entertainment in my room, but out of the way when I didn't want to see it. So, I included a retractable display with a lift for my TV. When needed, the screen ascends from its stand. If it's not in use, the TV disappears into its stand as if it was never there. With the bed facing the ocean, I only want to obstruct the scenic shoreline for moments at a time, and this technology allows me to do just that.

window seating

Throughout my life and travels I've been drawn to the design and layout of upscale hotel rooms. The best ones provide a nice balance of comfort and function. Within my bedroom, I wanted to make sure my calculated designs reimagined "casual" decor in the overall aesthetic. When I'm making moves, I am the consummate professional. But when I'm ready to relax, everything around me needs to encourage and promote that.

As the gorgeous ocean view was the primary draw for most everything regarding this home, window seating was both a preference and necessity. My mind typically has hundreds of thoughts, plans, projects, and to-dos running frantically through it 24/7. It's a zoo up there. But a tufted bench coupled with a quaint but sophisticated occasional table near the window ushers in quiet moments of reflection to help organize the day. With an active personal and professional life, I appreciate having small nooks to center myself and prepare for a full day over a cup of tea, or to assess the events of the workday in the evening. And for when my life doesn't run on schedule as I anticipated (because when does it ever?) I installed electrical outlets at the foot of my bed. My hectic work life involves having ever-ready, always-charged devices at my access, and this is a perfect way to achieve that when I'm getting ready in the mornings. Chaos is always looming in my world, but small conveniences and comfortable amenities in my bedroom help me stay centered and at one with myself.

primary bathroom

Traveling the world has always influenced who I am and what I do as a designer. Global persuasion can be seen throughout my home's design, and my primary bath is no different. As I created it, I leaned heavily into my international luxury hotel stays, especially ones I visited in Mexico. I loved the open layout of bedrooms and bathrooms with only a small plaster wall divider between them. It's a perfect visual balance of connection and separation, with elevated simplicity as the bonding base of the two spaces. With the blessing of an ocean oasis as the focus in the space, I wanted the bathroom to also face that direction and remain open. There is virtually no space in my bedroom that doesn't capture the magnificence of the ocean's splendor.

That said, the head of the bed serves as the nexus between the bathroom countertop, which, unconventionally, has two farmhouse sinks. I know, I know: those sinks are for kitchens! But are they, though? I wanted larger sinks in my bathroom, and the enameled cast-iron basins are versatile enough for any space. And they're huge! Why not put them in a bathroom? I installed one for myself and one for a potential future partner. Yes, I'm a single mother now, but I may not always be. The future should always be considered when creating a forever home. There's no harm in making room for what I want! I installed two brass Kallista showerheads because why not? The brass pops throughout the bathroom and accents the use of mixed metals in other rooms of the house. It's the perfect presentation of opulence at its finest!

No bathroom is complete without mirrors, but my space required something specific. I wanted three separate mirrors versus one large one. Why? A larger, traditional mirror would have disrupted those ocean views, and I wanted to maintain continuity anywhere I stood in my bedroom and bathroom. The custom floating, octagonal mirrors give me reflective perspectives from the front and sides, and they're spaced to offer the same amazing shoreline panorama as the bedroom. The mirrors are unlacquered brass, which will eventually oxidize and patina over time. It will maintain a classic look, both today and years from now.

soaking tub

The centerpiece of the primary bath brings in my affinity for metallics in interior design. I commissioned a custom Thompson Traders Quintana Tub with a satin brass finish for the space, and it is truly a shining star. Located directly under the skylight, it offers star-filled gazing during night soaks. Not only will the handcrafted tub provide unlimited moments of relaxation, but the evolving finish of the brass will continue to offer visual vibrance and personality to the bathroom for years to come.

primary closet

There's probably one word that could sum up my beach home's design: unorthodox.
But every decision was made with creativity and function in mind. That's not to say every
choice was easy to make. One of the more difficult design decisions involved my primary
closet space. I decided to make my "closet" its own separate room and intentionally
placed it on a different floor from my bedroom.

Of prime importance in my life as a designer and television personality is getting
dressed with a host of people handling various elements of preparation. There is
usually a makeup artist, a hair stylist, a fashion stylist, and most likely an assistant
running over the day's agenda and tasks. Oh, and the occasional kid asking questions
and eating snacks.

Preparing for events or media presentations is a production that comes with a great
deal of excited energy. I'd rather not have that in my private space of zen.

The social aspect of hair, makeup, and wardrobe in my closet dictated the layout and
amenities of the room. I have two makeup counters and an island with a seat built into
it. I installed mirrors around the room to ensure I'm presentable from all angles—a must
when your career requires extended time in front of the camera and under bright lights.
I also installed classic spherical mirror lights as an ode to Tinseltown. It's a small but
meaningful element that helps me tap into the spirit of Hollywood glam as I prepare for
events or TV appearances.

dressing area

You don't spend as much time in a makeup chair as I do without learning a thing or two about how light impacts your appearance. When I think about the long days of preparing for events and filming, I recall years of watching makeup artists hunting for adequate sunlight to get me camera-ready. I've watched many of them drag cumbersome lighting equipment into tight spaces to be able to ensure I look my best. Trust me, 4K camera clarity and harsh spotlights can be unkind to any human's imperfections, so I want to look amazing if someone's going to be photographing or filming me. My makeup chair was positioned with makeup artists in mind, facing the natural light that streams into this room. Additional vanity lighting that runs the length of the wall mimics the bright grandeur of old Hollywood, because classic glam is everything!

While having my face perfected for camera is one thing, the other part is accessorizing. I've used the same hair and makeup artist for years, and she has also served as my long-standing stylist. One of the last things we do in preparing my outfits is choose accessories. They are one of the few things I keep on display, especially the gold and silver, chunky and funky fashion jewelry. So much of my jewelry comes from antique shopping and my grandmothers' collections; the pieces all have visual stories to tell and memories that I always want to remain front and center. Having accents easy-to-reach for swapping in and out is a practical choice when creating great looks.

moroccan details

I'm a designer who believes that small design choices are just as important as major ones. I wanted every inch of my home to be purposefully created, which includes small details like the vent covers. The classical elements and craftsmanship of Moorish motifs are seen throughout my home and are reflected in this custom metalwork.

custom built-ins

While the overall closet design came from my creative needs, the dimensions of the space made some decisions for me. For instance, one area of this space is very shallow, which made it the perfect place for my shoe storage—practicality wins. Most of my clothing is behind mirrored doors, which I consider very calming. The reality of keeping up the hyper-organized and tidy look needed for open storage is completely unrealistic with my chaotic, grab-and-go type of schedule. I'd rather not have guests experience a pile of shoes or the occasional unhung garment when the closet door is open. Closed storage with beautiful interior cabinet lighting keeps everything orderly and always serene.

home office

Unconventional is a descriptor I'd say is pretty accurate for most parts of my life. My work life is no exception. At any given point in the year, I could have several clients' projects in progress, a TV show script to read over, and a product line of samples to approve. Life is a whirlwind for sure. That means I don't sleep much and I work a lot. Having a dedicated space to do all of that isn't just a luxury; it's an essential element that enhances my workflow.

My home office might be modest in size, but what it lacks in square footage it more than makes up for in efficiency. Located right outside the guest bedroom, this rectangular space is light and airy, mostly due to large windows that allow for ample ambient light.

Not one for wasting any bit of space, my custom wooden desk wraps around to span the length of the room. Life as a mom of two, a serial entrepreneur, and a passionate philanthropist can get messy, but my workspace doesn't have to be. Cabinetry under the desk is the gift that keeps on giving. Shelving extends to the ceiling, and I make great use of it with all my designer materials, rendering plans, and, of course, a bit of greenery to keep the space feeling organic and earthy. If you're going to spend a lot of time in a space, you'd better love it. This office feels comfortable, serene, and sufficient. Those are qualities and conditions anyone can thrive under when your goals are triumph and accomplishment. When I'm not in the air heading off to some other destination, this is where I go to get it all done.

boys' area

kingsley's bedroom

Interior designers spend a lot of time expressing their passion for beautifying spaces. I love discovering new ways of enhancing a home for the people who will interact with it most. It only makes sense, as our spaces are largely functional in nature. However, design isn't just meant to be used in the most literal sense. Our spaces can take on a sort of autobiographical role. Home emphatically represents personal canvases on which we paint our memories. Our homes all tell a story, so I'm intentional about selecting components that create an accurate narrative.

My approach to Kingsley's bedroom is no different. I wanted his room to reflect who he is, but in a way that felt organically and deeply about him. I had no clue that asking Kingsley about his preferences for his first solo room would lead to such a wonderfully weird request, but I'm so glad it did.

floating bed

Interior designers often work with renderings before details are finalized in a space. I created a bed for a virtual interior design project some time ago, and as is the case with many digitally designed items, it was by all accounts futuristic. The rendering made the bed appear as if it was floating. My ever-perceptive Kingsley took notice and asked if I would design it for his room. How could I say no?

I enlisted the help of a carpenter who could bring my vision to reality. We visited an authentic Moroccan furniture store, where Kingsley hand-selected the trim pieces that would serve as detail on the sides of the bed. If you're wondering if I was secretly bursting with joy at the thought of his palpable interest in each step of the design process, the answer is a resounding yes!

I reminisced on the very first piece I ever designed, which happened to be a bed. I requested a canopy bed for my eleventh birthday, so my mom took me to a store that made pieces out of iron. I can remember my excitement as I sketched out the ideas for my bed with the owner of the store. I had to wait a month for it to be constructed, but it was well worth it. My canopy bed always felt like a magical, safe haven during my teen years. So when Kingsley's eyes lit up as he described what he desired in his own custom bed, I recognized that feeling from my own experience.

The "floating bed" doesn't actually float. It's more of an optical illusion. The wooden bed frame is attached to a platform box that is bolted to the floor to prevent the entire thing from flipping over. There is mariner rope mixed with cleats and brass to give it the suspended-in-air appearance. The bed's natural light tone is a stark contrast against the navy room. Kingsley is young, but I deliberately decided on a king-sized bed with his growing stature in mind. I have always believed a child's bedroom should be able to grow with the child. The larger bed will ensure longevity in this space.

artistic grunge

Spend any amount of time in this part of California and you'll quickly realize that there's no escaping graffiti. It. Is. Everywhere. In fact, my childhood was filled with experiences and recollections of this flashy and stylized artful technique. My mother would often drive to Melrose Avenue when I needed updated photos for my modeling jobs. I remember slipping in and out of various ensembles from my wardrobe in the back alleys of this iconic stretch of road. One by one, I would pose against the backdrop of vibrant and expansive murals, each brought to life by the edgy art form. I might have been a cute, curly-haired tyke in colorful clothing, but there were two stars in those snap-shots, and one of them had nothing to do with me.

My sons and I travel frequently, both domestically and abroad, conversing about all the interesting similarities and differences in each city and country. We've all noticed that whether it's Madrid, London, Portland, or Paris, graffiti is present as a marker of artistic grunge. Well, those engaging conversations didn't fall on deaf ears. Kingsley was absorbing information like a sponge and was hard at work dreaming up his own plans for his future bedroom. Little did I know that the often underappreciated and misunderstood art form was about to get the VIP treatment in Kingsley's room.

With a foundation of graffiti and a goal of elegance, I paired graffiti by local artist Ruben Rojas with a wainscoting trim piece almost like you would see in a castle. I was confident the result wouldn't only be unique but stunning. I inlaid the panels with the customized graffiti instead of something more conventional like toile. I knew a monochromatic tonality would accentuate the art and refine the otherwise edgy visuals. Both the wainscoting and graffiti would be displayed in Kingsley's favorite color, blue, and this is the only room I chose to paint a true color.

elegant details

Like a suit paired with a T-shirt, juxtaposing the edginess of graffiti with leather-wrapped handles helped me maintain a level of sophistication that would ensure this room would grow with my son.

Attention to detail is what elevates a space. The raw Moroccan carvings on Kingsley's European-style desk echo the other cross-cultural elements throughout the home and offer a satisfying distinction.

a bathroom built for boys

Being a mom and a designer, creating a bathroom for young boys is about more than just having a space necessary for them to get clean (although that is *very* important). I'm concerned about their development. As this will be their private domain, I felt it important to make a space for them that expresses their personalities as well as facilitates their growth. Their new bathroom achieves that in some traditional and very non-traditional ways.

The boys' bathroom is one of the more voguish areas in the home; but that makes sense, seeing as they're the coolest kids in California. Both for the creative inspiration and audible applications, I believe they'll appreciate this space as kids and young adults.

Two challenges I had with the Jack and Jill bathroom involved the door and vanity. I chose a pocket door to save space. In a full gut renovation this is easy to add and allows access in and out that a swinging door would not. Because the bathroom is not large, I wanted a striking design with a minimalist touch. I'm confident I succeeded with that task.

As much as I want to help my children by giving them a head start in life, I also have to make sure they can take care of themselves when the time comes. Even at their age, I want to offer them opportunities to build responsibility into their daily lives. An easy way for them to do that (and not have my own clothing affected) is with laundry. I set up their bathroom with this in mind, so they are tasked with keeping their clothes clean. To their future life partners, you're welcome. I'll take my payment in grandkids.

designing for djs

A world without music is a world I wouldn't want to live in. That goes triple for my home, and I believe my boys would agree with me. If there were a way we could have every song everywhere all at once, we would! I tried my hardest to make that a reality as I built this home and infused music throughout the rooms, including the boys' bathroom.

My sons have been thriving with their extracurricular activities, including DJing. I began DJing as a young adult, and it's a skill I've enjoyed recreationally for a couple of decades. It was only a matter of time before my sons, dubbed DJ King and DJ Ken, developed a strong interest in music curation. I may be a bit biased, but I think they are both pretty good at it! As an homage to our family's love of music, I infused elements of mixing into their bathroom decor, in both the sights and sounds.

Anybody who's been to a Los Angeles club knows what to expect after crossing the velvet rope: flashes of strobing lights throughout a sea of obsidian, crowds completely enamored with the music and the moment, the energy of exclusivity filling the atmosphere. I wanted to appeal to that aesthetic, so their bathroom has that moody aura and presentation. In the shower area I utilized a bold Neolith stone called "Metropolitan" with a Steel Touch finish. The distressing in the stone cuts through with contrasting hints of gray and silver, providing a modern, cutting-edge appeal in the space. The rest of the shower hardware follows suit and complements the stone with matte black finishes, from the showerhead and hand shower to the mountings and hoses. VIP all the way, baby!

The Kohler Betello toilet in the color Black Black isn't the most conventional selection, but the choice works perfectly with the other design decisions, as does the lighting. I opted for low-voltage wiring for lighting around the mirror to allow a slight glow that is visible but won't be a distraction with brightness.

I continued the DJ motif with the prominent use of sphere-shaped decor. It was only right to incorporate that in the bathroom design, seeing as how they both use turntables and jog wheels on their digital music controllers. Finally, I included the Kohler Moxie speaker showerhead in their bathroom for maximum musical impact. They'll be able to wake up with tracks in their head to motivate them morning and night. I love that my budding DJs are the only ones in the house with this feature in their bathroom.

kensington's room

Designing for kids presents an especially unique challenge, because as the adult (and in this case, an expert on the children), we know best. But designing is about catering to the person—child or adult—who will live there. To succeed at gifting my youngest son with the room of his dreams, I enlisted the help of a visualization tool. In the beginning stages of building our dream home, I brought the boys to what was then a full-blown construction site. That probably sounds scarier than it was, but since my boys have been visiting worksites with me their entire lives, I knew they were on board.

   With only the beams of their rooms marking where walls would eventually live, I asked my sons to imagine where they would be a year from that day. Kensington (whom we call Kensi) is my youngest son. He is shy, athletically inclined, and has an incredible talent for drawing. I had my own guesses about what he might like, but I wanted him to describe what he envisioned for his future room. He closed his eyes and said he envisioned himself sketching. That simple request would go on to highly influence the design of his room.

window coverings

Kensi's custom window coverings feature leopard toile from my wallpaper and fabric collection. It was a conscious choice to install an element constructed with something I personally designed above the place where he would be creating on a regular basis. I designed the toile with my travels to Kenya in mind. It's a place filled with so much hope and promise. The women and girls I work to help in that region are as effervescent as they are tenacious. I see those same characteristics in Kensi. The print, in this location, felt intuitive.

overtly minimal

Clutter all but equals chaos, both in my mind and home. Every design choice in Kensi's room was aimed at creating a serene and simplistic zone to discourage disorder. In his moderately-adorned space, the texture of the intricate Moroccan carvings and island-esque aura of the louvered doors ensure visual charm and offer an attractive veneer behind which his things can be neatly stored. Doors and their artistic impact—often forgotten or at least disregarded in the design ideation process—are among the elements we interact with most, and they deserve great consideration.

the drawing desk

If you spend any extended amount of time with Kensi, you'll likely witness his disappearing act. Luckily for me, I know where he likes to hide. Kensi regularly seeks out time to disengage from the stimuli occurring around him to sit and sketch. Left to his own devices he can draw for hours, even if no one else is around. So, when we visited the Academy Museum of Motion Pictures in Los Angeles, it was no surprise that he was immediately enamored by the Disney drafting tables. His wide-eyed expression and sudden burst of energy provided all the evidence I needed to support what I already suspected: this was a passion.

Maybe it's because my own parents took my skills and talents seriously that I'm always watching my boys for insight or a potential peek into their future careers and life paths. For me, his enthusiasm was an opportunity to create something, a physical manifestation, that would show Kensi he and his gifts were seen, understood, and valued. That moment of fascination became the inspiration for his personal custom drawing desk. Was commissioning carpenters and furniture makers an expensive operation? Yes. Did I sometimes wonder if I'd lost my mind a bit during the process of bringing it all together? Again, yes. But when making an investment in my sons' development, there isn't a price on that.

Our museum visit emphasized the specialized dimensions and features required for efficient sketching. As such, Kensi's desk has a pencil holder shelf, sits at counter height, and pivots up or down to drafting angle. I paired it with an adjustable chair with a hand crank, an intentional choice for my more mechanical, engineering-minded son.

kids' playroom

My kids are never leaving this house. At least, that's my not-so-secret goal. I know that sounds crazy, but designing my forever home meant creating a space that would allow my favorite people to thrive. It just so happens that those little guys are quite vivacious—which is a nice way of saying my sons run on a never-ending supply of natural energy. Any dream home of mine better include plenty of outlets for those bouncing bambinos if I want to keep them as happy as I intend to be in our spaces.

I know my sons will grow up one day and leave the nest, but for now, I cherish all the moments we spend together. The unique additions I included, even the ones that pushed limits and made my contractor sweat, were all calculated. We are a home school hybrid family that spends a great deal of time with other families in our cohort. I wanted the playroom to give the kids a dedicated and separate area to entertain their friends, so much planning was allocated to the "entertainment ability" of our home.

Essentially, the boys wanted their own kids' living room. Every piece I selected was kid-friendly and kid-centered—including the seating. I chose funky-shaped, modular chairs that can be reconfigured in multiple ways. The best part is that the pieces are designed to be crawled on, so the kids can sit anywhere and any way they please. If I cave one day and allow gaming consoles, this is the perfect setup.

the treenet

Serenity isn't something most children think about, but it is a topic on the minds of many moms. When I saw the ocean views I would be privy to in this house, I knew right away that I wanted to feature them throughout, including in the playroom. I often integrate nature or elements that connect us to it in my design projects because of its calming ability. This mom craves a peaceful environment, so with two active preteen boys in one space, I wanted to create a custom design with them in mind. Putting my utopian dreams aside I decided to find a way to keep their bodies in motion and treat them to seaside sights at the same time.

To create a space that would entice and enchant my boys (because they needed to fall in love with this room) I pulled from moments in my motherhood journey. You know that feeling of beginning your day with high hopes and big plans only to see those intentions quickly go down the drain with one look at the rainy forecast? Parents do! The mad search for places like indoor gyms and libraries commences, because, well, how else are we supposed to keep our kids busy and stimulate their brains?

Our treenet was the answer for that conundrum. I hired The Treenet Collective, a team that specializes in creating custom treenets that they weave on-site. Our treenet is woven in a monochromatic gray rope material and suspended in the air. The kids can climb into it and pretty much do whatever they choose while they're up there!

rock wall and alcove

The treenet is cool, but the way you gain access to it is where the real fun begins! The kids climb a rock wall, something our family has enjoyed outside of the house many times and a highly requested detail from the boys. A sloped wall keeps the difficulty level kid-friendly.

multifunctional space

The idea of a playroom might seem limiting when you think of a forever home. The mark of a well-designed home is one that can flow with you through life transitions. That takes significant forethought, but the benefits are undeniably valuable. One such premeditated detail came in the form of having no doors. A doorless playroom means I never have to nag the kids about keeping the door open, something I hear parents of teenagers deal with often. Listen, kids will be kids, but nothing's stopping this mama bear from keeping a keen eye on her cubs!

The other detail that was a must was well-functioning desks. Our family is on a home school hybrid program, so having a dedicated place to study and get work done is crucial. The kids' workload will likely only increase as they age. These desks will grow with them while also ensuring this space remains uncluttered.

The two built-in desks have corkboards for any notes they need to keep handy, but the rest of the unit is a system of cabinets and drawers that enable all the boys' school items to be placed out of sight. An unusually shallow depth system allows for full utility of the desks while minimizing their impact on the rest of the space in the room.

music studio

Poets have called music the element that soothes savage beasts. Other artists have said it makes the world go 'round. For my family, it is a daily necessity for motivation and creativity. While we have the baby grand piano in the living room, I created a recording studio for the boys on the lower level behind the guest apartment—*far*, far away from Mommy's peaceful dwelling.

Complete with computer and audio monitors, a keyboard/audio controller, electronic drum pads, and a DJ setup, the space is a music maker's dream! My sons DJ in LA and Ibiza, and they've shown an interest in producing and remixing tracks. This space allows them the resources to continue growing their musical expressions and talents.

playroom bathroom

The bathroom is one of the first things you see when you enter the playroom, so in my opinion, "fabulous" was more essential than elective. I made it a statement with a gorgeous integrated stone sink with a boxy, modern form. People tend to underestimate that stone and simply read it as elegant, but it's also fairly indestructible. Due to its wipeable exterior, it's easy to keep clean. This bathroom is also available for guests, thus it tows the line of practical and sophisticated. A more traditional French gold European-style faucet balances out the modern sink. Juxtaposing design restraint with over-the-top maximalism, the giant chandelier is right on time in this otherwise minimal room—and it's too high for my boys to swing from!

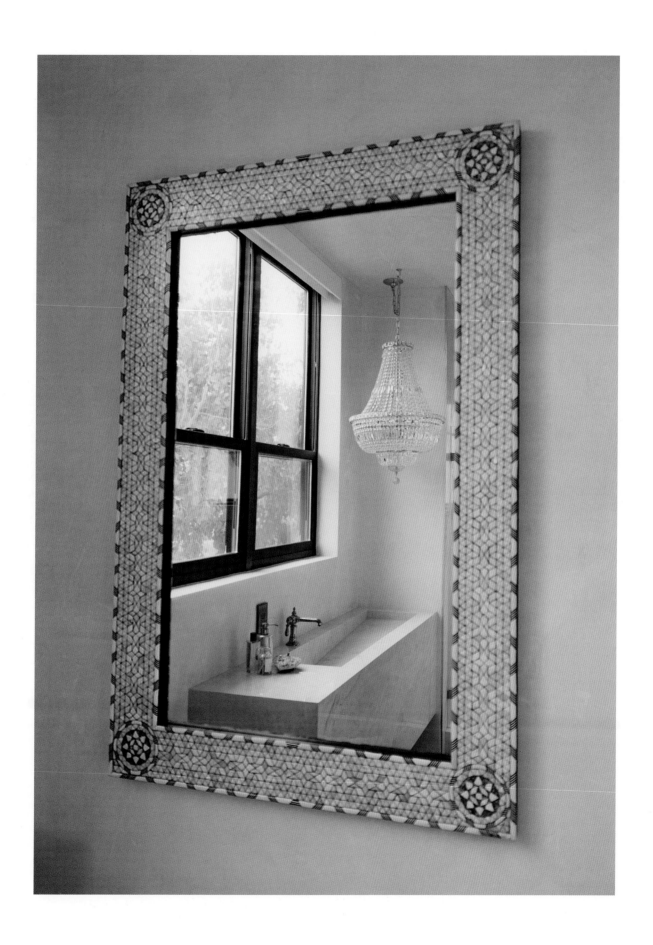

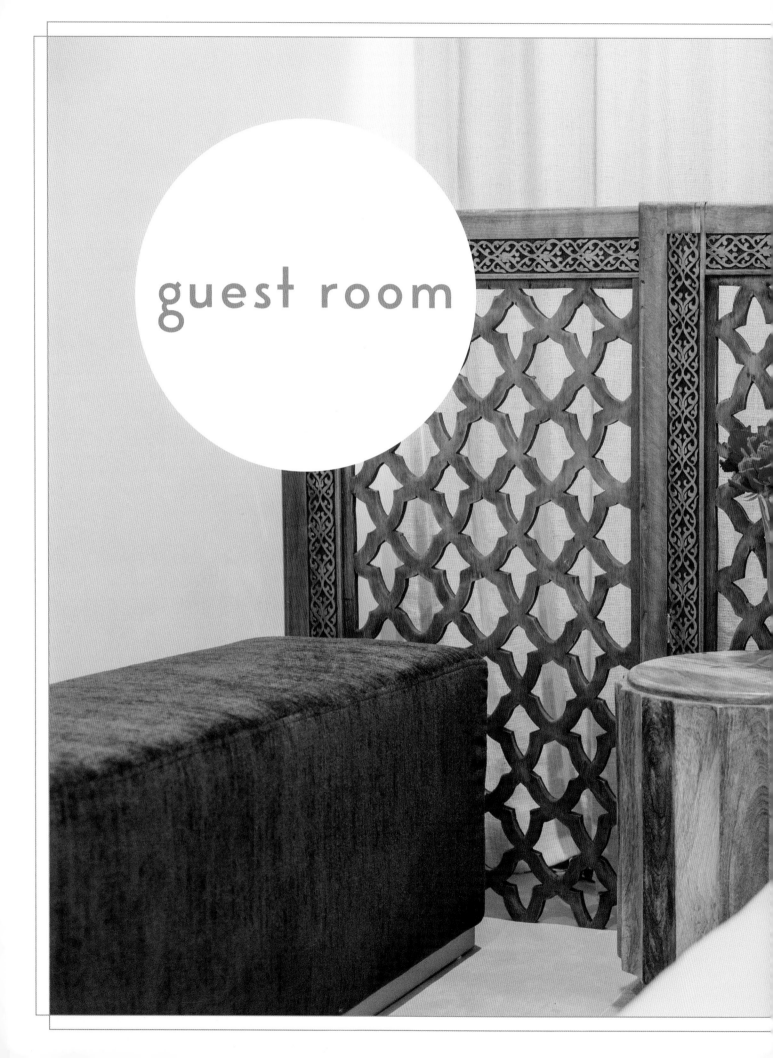

guest room

If all our days culminate in an orchestral masterpiece that fills life with immeasurable beauty, then the people we live it with are the music notes. In many cultures the family structure involves much more than just the nuclear unit. It often includes grandparents, aunts and uncles, and even close friends. My younger self would never have believed my inner circle would be so large, but my friends, who hail from almost every corner of the earth, enrich my life with their love for my kiddos and me. They are my village, and this cherished group was absolutely considered in the building of my home.

Since my goal is to keep my loved ones close as long as possible, I knew I would need to design a room so beautiful that they wouldn't want to leave. My guest bedroom is undeniably tropical. One of the most prominent details is a mural wallpaper from my own line that features hand-painted lush jungle vegetation reminiscent of what you'd find on the beaches of the Indian Ocean. Vibrant hues of green, pink, gold, and teal span the length of a wall and make the space feel more like a staycation escape.

I'm a woman who defines luxury in diverse ways—one of which revolves around life's simple conveniences. The emerald-green bench on a wall adjacent to the bed provides a proper spot for guests to place their luggage when they arrive and also serves as seating.

lattice headboard

The custom headboard has a Moroccan lattice-inspired design. Behind the headboard are automated window coverings, perfect for undisturbed sleep after a long flight. Arched pocket doors are the final touch in this mini getaway. Thoughtful, personalized, and effective, my guest bedroom remains primed for all the visiting friends who I can convince to stay awhile with my little family.

guest bathroom

We all have our "icks"! One of mine just happens to be private sounds that somehow make it into public ears. I'm not interested in hearing or being heard when bathroom matters are in session. Directly outside of the guest bedroom is the entrance to the guest bathroom, which is home to a sizable, green-tile Moroccan fountain with a gold spout. The sound of running water provides both soothing white noise and acoustic disguise. The deep green color is complemented by wainscoting and a chair rail design with "Palmyra" wallpaper from my collection.

materials moment

No design of mine is complete without a mixed metals moment. Consequently, the
sink, mirror, and two sconces all boast a vivid brass finish, while the shower showcases
a nickel showerhead and controls. The polished stone shower walls with green
undertones are the perfect pairing with the grassy shades in this space.

apartment

I have always believed women can have it all and do it all. However, the process of procuring the "all" is significantly easier when you tackle it with a support team. That's why I never hesitated to employ a live-in au pair when my kids were younger. I wanted the security of knowing my children weren't lacking while mom went out to build an empire. Think about it: Batman had Robin, Snoopy had Woodstock, Shrek had Donkey . . . you get it. Teamwork makes the dream work!

My children are a bit older now, and while we don't have an au pair, I realize that none of us can predict the time we might possibly need a space for a family member to live with us for an extended period. When that time comes, you'll want to give them their own space—for their sanity and yours. This additional unit downstairs has its own separate keyless entry, a plus for privacy. It is a mini apartment and was paramount in my quest to future-proof my home.

This space is a bit of a tribute to my travels and has been embellished with many pieces from my fabric and wallpaper line. I customized the bed with the "Kisumu" print, a safari toile, as the headboard and footboard fabric. There are two custom accent chairs in my "Pokot" print, which is a spice-colored leopard pattern. There is even a richly hued rug that I picked up on a trip to Morocco. With the travel theme highlighted throughout this space, I made a deliberate choice to mix and match the hardware to highlight this feeling of wanderlust.

bold kitchenette

The kitchenette is feature-rich with black and gold appliances as attractive as they are functional. I adore a serene color palette in kitchen spaces, so the boldly colored range, hood, and refrigerator are paired with a stone that can only be described as striking. The Calacatta Luxe stone is the star of the space with golden, ochre, and gray veining on a white backdrop. With so much of the kitchenette falling on the neutral side of the spectrum, I had no issue integrating strong patterning with the background surfaces in the room. Creating beauty often requires a "no holds barred" approach.

luxe bathroom

What's an apartment without a proper bathroom? A dose of Calacatta Royale stone, golden accents, and crystal give this space an Old Hollywood glamour touch. The stone selection was inspired by classic Italian marble, a deliberate choice, as I wanted the space to have an old-world feel while still maintaining a timeless quality. The all-in-one vanity has stone integrated with a gold faucet and controls. An aged-brass and crystal wall light augments the Hollywood feel.

rooftop

It's no secret that I love Southern California. I cannot imagine living anywhere else in the U.S. That doesn't mean it doesn't have a few challenges when it comes to real estate. Other regions of the country get sprawling green lawns in the spring and technicolor leaves that feel like something out of a movie in autumn. We, on the other hand, have tall and narrow houses with limited acreage.

But save your pity.

What Angelenos lack in lot radius is outweighed by near-perfect weather year-round and majestic beaches—a central design feature for my home. Perhaps no other space wholly benefits from the true sensory experience of our ocean-adjacent abode like the rooftop. Those splendid sea and shore views and vibes are the main characters of my rooftop, and my mission was to ensure they completely stole the show.

enhanced views

We experience life with all our senses, even when we're not keenly aware of it. The rooftop organically benefits from an exceptional factor: the ocean. But why stop there? I enlisted the help of a professional who could bring the ideas in my head to fruition. I wanted to cover the outdoor ceiling with flowing fabric to emulate ocean waves. This choice of adornment was ideal for complementing an alfresco environment in a way that offers shade while still allowing the right amount of sun to shine through. See, I didn't just want to enhance the beauty of the rooftop; I wanted to create a space that feels like an encounter with nature. The rooftop isn't just another space, it is a highlight—a part of my home that I hope will become a prominent spot for my family and guests.

With the shoreline a simple glimpse away and salty ocean air wafting through the space, my rooftop practically feels like an extension of the beach. Nature was determined to upstage every other detail in the very best way, and I wanted to capitalize on that. Infusing the area with natural decor felt intuitive.

I selected pieces from Phillips Collection, a brand recognized for their global style and organic but modern furnishings. I adorned the space with three substantially sized stone pieces made of natural crushed stone in a Roman Stone finish. The oversized stone sculpture is positioned in a corner of the rooftop adjacent to the Jacuzzi, perfect as an ocean lookout. A wide-seat bench flanks the Jacuzzi on the other side. An organically shaped coffee table is an ideal complement to the nature-centric seating area, complete with rounded rattan chairs, a smaller occasional table, and an armless concrete chair. In line with the minimalist theme of the rooftop, I opted for bar-height bistro tables. Everyone tends to congregate around them at parties, and you always need a place to set your beverage or plate. This space is primed for a good time!

entertainment essential

Most of the work in designing a lounge or entertainment space is in the basic factors that are more atmospheric than they are aesthetic. The rooftop has a marine-grade TV for movie night along with a complete sound system, but the beauty is in the wiring! Listen, if you're going to claim to be everyone's favorite always-party-ready gathering spot, you'd better have the tunes that keep bodies dancing all night—or at least until everyone is worn out and ready to go to bed. Speakers are connected to everything in the house, but I was deliberate about wiring them from the DJ booth to the roof independently. No matter what's going on and where it's happening, the party (and the after-party) will never be without a proper soundtrack.

jacuzzi and deck

I'm not sure if anything proves my love for my water-loving family like having a Jacuzzi lifted by crane and placed on the roof! It was quite the undertaking, but for us, the result was worth it. In line with other parts of the house and keeping the view within view, I wanted the Jacuzzi to be above ground and have the height so you could sit inside and look out at the ocean.

When you're a designer who prefers bespoke design but loves incorporating more economical methods to achieve it, you get creative! I decided on a prefabricated Jacuzzi with an accompanying built-in bench to accommodate seating. Strategically positioned MoistureShield decking around the tub makes the space feel cohesive and sleek, but that's not its only advantage!

Fellow Californians will tell you a million times how much they love the generous amount of sunshine and warmth we enjoy year-round. Californian parents will tell you that the beautiful weather means our tireless kiddos have that much more time to expend energy outside—an invaluable benefit, if I do say so myself. With that perk in mind, I prioritized decking that would be suitable for little feet when the forecast features those higher temperatures. The decking choice is heat and splinter resistant, making a safer place for the kids' antics, and it gives mama the appearance of a custom hot tub without the cost of one.

wet room

When it comes to fun and celebrations, I'm a "go big or go home" kind of girl. If it's not already painfully obvious, we take entertaining seriously in our household. Whether you're gathering with just a few family members or commemorating a major occasion, the key to having a successful time is to ensure your space can accommodate it. For me, that included one of the essential elements needed at any and every party: a bathroom!

This is what I affectionately refer to as the party bathroom. This jewel box of a bathroom is on the rooftop just steps away from the Jacuzzi. I designed this bathroom to function more like a wet room, meaning every square foot of it is water safe. The surfaces aren't delicate, but they are beautiful! It takes only a single glance to be captivated by the Moroccan-inspired glazed terra-cotta tile in a brilliant teal. The sparkle of the Ibizan sea as sunrays bounce about over its rippling waves has long had me under its spell. This customized tile in a hexagon shape at double size is an ode to that unmatched majesty.

The mom in me knows that my sons and their friends will find a way to create a mess no matter where they are. The entire bathroom can be easily hosed down and sanitized, which makes cleanup after events (and after my sons and their crew of friends splash everywhere!) exceptionally simple. It's a smaller space, so I eliminated the need for separation by glass. The golden accents provide a jewelry-like accent against the deep nautical hue. The rooftop is a sight to see, but this bathroom is pretty extraordinary in its own right.

my sincerest gratitude

There are so many people who were pivotal in helping me create this home. In no particular order, I want to say thank you to:

Mom and Dad for always allowing me to soar and for supporting my talents and dreams throughout my life. I love you beyond what words will ever be able to relay.

Brian Samuels, for your management expertise and for being a really great friend.

Courtney Pisarik for ideating this project and pushing to make it happen.

Team Breegan Jane, both past and present: you know who you are. You are forever a part of this, and I'm grateful for your contributions.

Beyoona Photography and Katee Grace for always capturing beautiful moments of my family.

Leslie and the Savoy House team for expanding my thoughts as a designer and working tirelessly to launch my collection.

The talented Clarke & Clarke, Sanderson Design Group, and Kravet Inc. teams for helping me craft a gorgeous fabrics and wallpapers collection.

Ruben Rojas for your simple but powerful message of love that will always be a part of our lives.

To all the vendors who helped me create this one-of-a-kind forever home:

Ty Bergman, Customline Woodworking, South Side Electric, AJ's Glass, Renewal by Andersen, JennAir, Trane, GAD Art & Fabrication, Thompson Traders, Neolith, JT and Paco for your amazing handwork with all our stone design, MoistureShield, Phillips Collection, Emtek, Arts Out Of Africa, DJ 4tify, Feizy Rugs, The Tile Bar, The Shade Store, Furnitureland South, Badia Design Inc., Jeanne K Chung, Brad Angeleri, Ty Cueva, Barry Roach, California Closets, Kohler, Kallista, The Treenet Collective, Hello Sunshine Surf Racks, the Los Angeles Public Library, and Tyka Pryde and your design team for the great styling and design support. Most of all, I'd like to thank Fabian Soria and his team, the real hands who molded this house into a home.

To the team that helped bring this publication to fruition:

Terrence and Kristin, my "A" Squad, who have been helping me write the stories of my life for almost a decade: we made this book a reality, and I'm so proud of us!

Ryan Garvin, thank you for photographing every piece of beauty since the beginning of my career.

Carisha Swanson, thank you for putting your stamp on this book as a respected industry leader.

Madge Baird, I'm grateful to you for compiling all of the elements of this amazing book so beautifully.

I am eternally appreciative for all of your creativity and support. Thank you.

about the author

Designer, author, and philanthropist Breegan Jane showcases her vast expertise building homes, designing products, and hosting television shows, all while balancing life as a single mother. Breegan's successful career as a television host, spanning over a decade across several networks, reveals her prolific talent for storytelling. Her global influence in interior design can best be seen in her product lines available in the United States, Africa, and Europe, establishing her as a globally recognized brand.

Breegan is a lifestyle influencer who regularly travels between Ibiza and Los Angeles. She participates heavily in traveling speaker series and keynote presentations, boldly asserting the possibility of achieving success in both career and personal endeavors. Humanitarian projects take a charitable priority in Breegan's life. She dedicates her time to working to eliminate FGM around the world.

First Edition

29 28 27 26 25   5 4 3 2 1

Text © 2025 Breegan Jane

Photograph credits as follows:

© 2025 Ryan Garvin: cover front and back; 2 inset, 6–7, 14, 20, 21, 22–3, 26–7, 29, 30, 33, 34, 35, 37, 38, 40, 43, 46–7, 49, 50, 54–5, 58–9, 61, 62–3, 64, 65, 66, 68, 70–1, 73, 74–5, 77, 78–9, 82, 85, 86–7, 88, 89, 90, 91 T & B, 93, 94, 96–7, 98, 99, 102, 104–05, 106–07, 108, 111, 112 R, 114, 119, 120–21, 122, 123, 125, 126, 128, 129, 132, 133, 135 TR & BR, 137, 139, 141, 143, 144–45, 148, 152–53, 154–55, 156–57, 160, 162, 163, 168, 169, 170–71, 175, 176, 177, 178, 179, 180–81, 183, 185, 186, 189, 191, 192–93, 195, 196–97, 198, 200–01, 202, 207, 208–09

© 2025 Beyoona Photography: 32, 41, 45 T & B, 51, 52, 53, 57, 67, 81, 101, 110, 112 L, 113, 116–17, 130, 135 L, 136, 138, 142, 146–47, 148, 149, 150, 151, 159, 164, 165, 166 67, 172, 184, 190, 194, 205, 206

© 2025 Katee Grace: 4_5, 11, 13 all, 15, 16 all

Courtesy Breegan Jane: 8, 76

Courtesy Breegan Jane and Clarke & Clarke Collection: back cover; borders on front cover, 1, 2, 28, 56, 80, 136, 142, 182, 194

Courtesy Eyre Powell Chamber of Commerce Collection / Los Angeles Public Library: 22-23 (enlarged photo)

Artwork © 2025 Ruben Rojas: 120–21, 122, 123, 125, 126, 129, 130, 132

Published by

Gibbs Smith

570 N. Sportsplex Dr.

Kaysville, Utah 84037

1.800.835.4993 orders

www.gibbs-smith.com

Designed by Rita Sowins / Sowins Design

Printed and bound in China

Product is made of FSC®-certified and other controlled materials.

MIX
Paper | Supporting responsible forestry
FSC® C153458

Library of Congress Control Number: 2024943044

ISBN: 978-1-4236-6726-1